THE TALKS

A parent's guide to critical
conversations about sex, dating
and other unmentionables.

DVD STUDY GUIDE

BARRETT AND JENIFER JOHNSON

**INFO FOR
FAMILIES**
resources

© 2016 by Barrett and Jenifer Johnson

An INFO for Families Resource

www.infoforfamilies.com

Printed in the United States of America

All rights reserved. No part of this publication may be reproduced, stored in a retrieval system, or transmitted in any form or by any means – for example, electronic, photocopy, recording – without the prior written permission of the copyright holder. The only exception is brief quotations in printed reviews.

If you make copies of this workbook for your group without the author's permission, you are stealing. So please don't do that. You can find a reasonably priced download version at www.infoforfamilies.com/resources. If you would like to request free copies for your group, please contact INFO for Families directly.

All scripture quotations, unless otherwise indicated, are taken from the Holy Bible, New International Version®, NIV®. Copyright ©1973, 1978, 1984, 2011 by Biblica, Inc.™ Used by permission of Zondervan. All rights reserved worldwide. The "NIV" and "New International Version" are trademarks registered in the United States Patent and Trademark Office by Biblica, Inc.™

ISBN-13: 978-1518628870

This study is dedicated to any parent

who feels overwhelmed with the task

(but who is pretty confident that God is not).

CONTENTS

INTRODUCTION

Welcome to The Talks! We're so glad you've chosen to work through this study. Whether you're doing it on your own or with a group, our hope and prayer is that it will help you feel better equipped to tackle an intimidating dimension of parenting.

We want to start with a potentially awkward statement:

"We want our kids to experience great sex." It's strange, but true.

God made our kids (and yours) as sexual beings with the unique capability to connect powerfully and beautifully with another person. But we live in a world where many people get sex wrong. What God designed to be wonderful becomes the source of their greatest hurts.

We desperately want our kids to get it right.

Back in May, 2011, I read a report by Glenn T. Stanton that solidified my perspective on this. Perhaps it will bring about a paradigm shift in you, as well. He referenced a study by Professor Anthony Paik of the University of Iowa that looked specifically at the first sexual experiences of adolescents. Paik explained that his "research shows that adolescent sexuality/premarital sex is associated with marital dissolution." He found that females whose first sexual encounter was in their teen years had roughly double the risk of divorce once they married. Read that again. Paik's research suggests that sexually active teens are significantly crippling their ability to be successful in marriage. That is huge.

As I have worked with young married couples for the past decade, I have come to realize that much of the brokenness in the area of married sexuality got started in them long before marriage. For many, the experiences and mistakes of the teen years made for a dramatically compromised foundation on which to build a healthy marriage and sex life. The result is that what God designed to be an amazing dimension of adult life ends up being an issue of pain and regret.

And I am tired of picking up the pieces.

In a variety of contexts over the past few years, we have taught parents on the subject of sexuality. For the record, it hasn't been about how to do it (our assumption is that if a couple has biological children, they at least know the basics) but about how to help their kids to not mess it up in their own lives.

As we tackle these issues, the masses of people we have taught have been more stunned than anything. We have seen deer-in-the-headlights looks from many. We have invited them to consider a perspective that they, up to now, may have never heard before. For them, our prayer is that they would continue to talk about it, study the issues, and ask God for His insights into their kids and their unique situations. It has been a tremendous joy to hear the stories of parents becoming more intentional and the difference it is making in their families.

Please note: this is a difficult subject with few easy answers. There are some good principles that should guide us, but there are few hard and fast rules that are applicable to every family. As you watch the DVD's we'll give some "best practices, but you will not hear us offering any firm guarantees of any outcome.

Our goal is to encourage people to carefully consider the long-term effects of how they are leading and protecting their kids. And to make sure that God is involved in their choices.

Even if some of the topics aren't relevant to you because of your kids' ages, we hope you will glean something from each session. If it's not helpful to you, perhaps it will be helpful to someone you know.

Most importantly, we encourage you to wrestle with God on this stuff. The good thing about wrestling with Him is that you have to be in close contact with Him. That's always a good thing. Because He has a perspective on these issues and He wants you to look to Him for direction and help as you address them with your kids. The good news is that He is always with you!

Whether your kids are 6 or 16, the clock is ticking. May we join God in helping our kids discover (in the right way and in the right time) just how amazing He made sex to be.

-Barrett and Jenifer Johnson

HOW TO USE THIS STUDY GUIDE

Included in this resource are a couple of things that will help you to digest the content and make some meaningful real-life application in your home.

LISTEN

First of all, each session contains a note taking guide to help you to follow along. Along with key concepts, there are some blanks to fill in to make sure you don't fall asleep during the videos. (We'll put those key points on the screen so you don't miss them.) In addition, there is plenty of blank space so you can scribble down any insights that you feel are particularly helpful.

DISCUSS

Every section also includes a small group discussion guide. We feel that these truths are best processed with other people, so we hope you're working through it with a group of other like-minded parents. We have provided some questions to ponder as well as some scriptures to examine. Our prayer is that God will speak to you through His Word and other people in your faith community.

APPLY

This is your place to respond and become purposeful in equipping your kids to navigate our hyper-sexualized culture. For each session, we have offered a few suggestions but we have also left some room for you to identify your own action steps. Some of them will need to happen immediately, while others may be for much later. Because of that, we have included a "When?" column so you can stay on task both now and in the future.

MORE

Finally, we have included some suggestions of resources for further study. These are books, websites, and even some technology that might help you to be better equipped to tackle some of the issues that are introduced.

Finally, for those looking for us to boil it down to the absolute basics, we have included an appendix in the back of this guide with some simple checklists about what your kids might need to know about sex and relationships at different developmental stages. They aren't hard and fast rules (every family is unique), but they might give you a place to start.

Session 1
A Parent's Responsibility

"Your Kids Are Counting on You"

LISTEN

A Snapshot of our Hyper-Sexualized culture:

- The *typical adolescent in the US will view nearly 14,000 sexual references per year.*

- The average age of first time exposure to porn is 11.

- According to Chap Clark of the Fuller Youth Institute:"60% of our teen boys are addicted to porn, with addiction being defined as 3 visits to a porn site a week at an hour per visit."

- By the time they turn 19, 70% of teenagers have had oral sex.

- A recent study showed that, despite their behaviors, 90% of adolescents "agree that most young people have sex before they are really ready."

- "When a woman had premarital sex with just one partner before her spouse, she tripled the risk of divorce when compared with those who married as virgins."
  – Jay Teachmnan

7

It is a _____ job to help their kids navigate their sexuality.

A Parent's Checklist for Getting Ready to Tackle These Issues With Your Kids:

1. You have to have your child's _____.

2. Stop making _____.

   *Nobody _____ it for you.

   *You feel like a _____.

   *You are afraid to _____ your kids out.

   *The _____ dimensions of modern sexuality overwhelm you.

   *Your current _____ _____ is a mess.

3. Stop looking for an easy _____.

4. Get both _____ on the same page.

DISCUSS

In a 2012 study by the National Campaign to Prevent Teen Pregnancy, teens were asked who was most influential in their personal decisions about sex. Of those studied, 87% believe it would be easier for teens to postpone sexual activity if they were able to have more open, honest conversations about these topics with their parents.

Questions to Consider

Q. Did any of the statistics at the beginning of the video (see page 7) surprise you? Which ones?

Q. On a scale of 1-10, how comfortable do you feel talking about sexual issues with your kids?

Q. Can you relate to any of the "excuses" mentioned in the video? Which ones? Why?

Scripture to Examine

In Ezekiel 16, God tells a story about how He has cared for his people. It serves as an excellent picture of how parents must lead and guard their kids within our hostile cultural environment. Here's the background:

A child is born in secret and then abandoned in a field. The baby girl is left alone to die. God saw that the baby was unloved and alone and had intense pity for her. From that moment, God took responsibility for her life and her well-being, speaking life and blessings on her, just as a good parent naturally does. The story goes on to say that the girl eventually matured sexually. The Bible says that her breasts were formed and her hair grew long and beautiful, yet she was still naked.

"Later I passed by, and when I looked at you and saw that you were old enough for love, I spread the corner of my garment over you and covered your naked body." -Ezekiel 16:8

God models for parents the kind of care and protection that our kids need. When their bodies begin to mature and their hearts begin to awaken to love, our children need safeguarding, not unbridled freedom to explore their new awareness.

Our kids need someone to tell them that sex is awesome. They need someone who can cast a vision for how great it will be for them to enjoy it within the safe, committed environment of marriage some day. They need someone who will try to protect them from messing it up or doing it for all the wrong reasons.
That job belongs to us. We are their parents.

Q. Have you been guilty of counting on the school or the church to help your kids have a healthy understanding of sexual issues? Why or why not?

Q. If parents today are going to do what God did for the girl in Ezekiel 16:8, what issues might we need to address? What are some of the challenges our kids are going to face while growing up in this culture?

Conclude your small group time by praying for protection for your kids and for wisdom and intentionality for you. We desperately need God to help us with this!

For Additional Study

Read Deuteronomy 6:6-7 to see the directive that God gives to parents (not the church) about teaching God's ways.

Check out Malachi 4:6 and Luke 1:17 for details on the importance of having our kids' hearts.

APPLY

	What I am going to do:	**When:**

- Discuss with my spouse how we can begin to become more intentional. _____

- Find out what my kids are leaning about sexuality in school and church. _____

- Ask God to reveal any wrong beliefs about sex from my own developmental years. _____

- Give an honest evaluation of if I have the hearts of my kids. _____

- _____ _____

- _____ _____

- _____ _____

MORE

Books to Read:

Forbidden Fruit: Sex and Religion in the Lives of American Teenager by Mark Regnerus is an outstanding overview of our the world our kids are growing up in.

What are You Waiting For? by Dannah Gresh outlines beautifully the "why" of saving sex for marriage.

The Invisible Bond by Barbara Wilson helps adults break free from their sexual past.

Other:

The Five Love Languages is a great starting place to help you connect with the hearts of your kids. Find out more at www.5lovelanguages.com

The Flag Page is another tool to help you to understand how to love and relate to your kids. Go to flagpage.com.

Session 2

Having "The Talk"

"It's More Than One Conversation, But It Starts Here"

LISTEN

Knowing what to do and when to do it is a parenting stress most people can relate to. While it will never be easy, there are some principles to help you to get this right.

Develop a strategy for before, during, and after The Talk.

Before The Talk...

1. Model healthy _____.

2. Do your best to guard and protect your child's _____.

   *Stay on top of what they see.

   *Be diligent about who they interact with.

*Teach them how to guard against abuse.

3. Look for _____ that they are ready.

*You want your kids to hear about sex from you before they hear it from somebody else.

During The Talk...

1. At first, _____ talk to sons; _____

talk to daughters.

2. Make it a part of something monumental and

_____.

3. Keep it _____ _____.

4. Do" _____ " with your kids.

5. _____ before you preach.

6. Be _____! It is a miracle!

7. Ask your child to _____ to what you tell him.

After the Talk:

1. _____ back in with them.

2. The _____ parent should eventually enter the conversation.

3. Be_____.

4. Gear up for more _____.

DISCUSS

Nothing strikes fear into the heart of a parent like the thought of having to share the details of sexual intercourse with their children. Figuring out when to do it and how much to share is perhaps the hardest part.

Questions to Consider

Q. What memories (good and bad) do you have of your parents having "the talk" with you?

Q. If the goal is to make sure that your kids hear about "the birds and the bees" from you before they hear it somewhere else, what age do you think might be right for your kids? Do you feel like you are already behind schedule?

Q. What might be some "signs" that your child is ready?

Scripture to Examine

There is no perfect formula for getting this right. Every child and circumstance is different. When it comes to timing, Christ followers must depend on the leadership of God in our lives. He wants to help us to get this right. The good news is that He promises to lead us if we will only look to Him for direction.

"Whether you turn to the right or to the left, your ears will hear a voice behind you, saying, 'This is the way; walk in it.'" - Isaiah 30:21

As much as these issues might freak us out, we must realize that they do not freak God out. Remember: God invented sex! We can boldly ask God to give us conviction through His Holy Spirit regarding when we are to speak to our children about His design for sex.

"My sheep listen to my voice; I know them, and they follow me." - John 10:27

This leadership from God applies to timing but it also applies to what and how we share about sex. In those moments when we might feel tongue-tied or flustered given the things we are talking about, God wants to lead us. He wants to bring to our minds the right words and illustrations that will be meaningful to our kids. Does mean that it won't be awkward? Of course not. It's always going to be awkward. But we must trust God to help us.

Q. Does it feel strange asking God for help in talking about sex with your kids? If it does, what do you think that says about your own personal beliefs about God and sex?

Q. Is it hard for you to believe that He created it for our good? Is it difficult to grasp that talking about sex doesn't embarrass Him like it might embarrass you? Why or why not?

Q. Does this discussion leave you feeling with a sense of urgency? Why or why not?

Conclude by challenging each other in your group to get a plan for having "The Talk" with your kids. If your kids are older (10+) and it hasn't happened yet, then you will likely need to become VERY intentional. If your kids are younger, you can begin talking about what you might do in the future. Close by praying for courage and confidence for all of us as parents.

For Additional Study

Check out Genesis 2:24-25 for a reminder that God has created sex to be a glorious and shame-free gift for us within marriage

Read Isaiah 40:11 for some encouraging words about God's love and provision for parents who are leading young children.

APPLY

What I am going to do: When:

- Make a plan to have "the talk" with my
  kids who are of an appropriate age.   _____

- Go back to my older kids and "shore up"
  any parts of "the talk" that we did poorly.   _____

- Remind my kids that I am willing and
  available to talk about sexual issues.   _____

- _____   _____

- _____   _____

- _____   _____

MORE

Books to Read:

Point Man by Steve Farrar has an entire chapter devoted to having "the talk" and even provides a "script" you can use.

Passport to Purity audio series published by FamilyLife is a set of audio clips you can listen to with your kids on a weekend away.

God's Design for Sex published by NavPress and *Learning About Sex for the Christian Family* (Boys and Girls Editions) by Concordia are developmental book series you can use over many years.

The Chicken's Guide to Talking Turkey with your Kids About Sex by Kevin Leman is another great overview resource.

Videos to Watch:

"Simple Truths" by Mary Flo Ridley is a presentation that might be a help to parents having "The Talk." Find out more at www.maryflo.org

Session 3

The Impact of Social Media

"The Implications of Our Kids' Connections"

LISTEN

Social media is not going away. It has changed everything.

Constant connection means constant _____.

Social media is a major player as it relates to our kids' sexuality.

A Primer on Emotional Purity:

Most kids will not become sexually intimate until they first become _____ intimate.

Social media has the power to fast-track emotional

_____.

You are allowed to put _____ on your kids'
use of social media.

Plant this into their young minds as early and as often as possible!

1. Parameters on _____ they use social media.

2. Parameters on how _____ they use it.

3. Parameters on who they connect with in the

_____ world.

4. Parameters on _____ they say and do online.

A final word:

Don't put off the _____ _____
conversation.

   *Teach your kids to be careful about what they say online.

   *Tell your kids about the dangers of "sexting."

*Remind your kids that schools and employers regularly look at social media.

DISCUSS

Technological advances over the past decade have dramatically changed how we interact with others. While parents are working to integrate social media into their lives, the next generation has no knowledge of a world without it. In many homes, this results in a communication disparity. Kids are connecting with others mainly through social media while parents are desperately trying to figure out how it all works. While there are many issues we could examine related to our kids and their online connections, we want to look most closely at the implications of social media on our kids' sexual behaviors.

Questions to Consider

Q. What challenges have you faced trying to place parameters on your kids' use of social media? What has worked or not worked?

Q. If "constant connection means constant influence," how does that impact us as we parent our teenagers?

Q. Have you ever considered the connection between emotional intimacy and sexual intimacy? In your own experience growing up, do you think that they are connected? Why or why not?

Scripture to Examine

Tucked within the pages of Song of Solomon is a wonderful piece of advice that would serve our kids well. In this sometimes racy book that shares the intimate words sung between lovers, we read the following words on several different occasions:

"Do not arouse or awaken love until it so desires." –Song of Solomon 2:7, 3:5, 8:4

The entire book is devoted to describing the intense love and passion that is being experienced between the two lovers. It is like a wild beast that, once awakened, cannot be tamed. In that context, Solomon is both describing the powerful force that he and his bride now know AND he is warning others not to go there until they are absolutely ready to handle it. The emotion is so powerful, intoxicating, and life-changing, you better not unleash it until you are ready. Because once you awaken it, it's near impossible to turn it off.

Our culture encourages our kids to awaken it as soon as possible...and as often as possible. Unfortunately, social media gives them endless chances to let their guard down.

Q. What might you do to begin to train your kids on the issue of "emotional purity?"

Q. What are some best practices that parents can use to monitor their kids' social media use? (See the list of "parameters" on page 22 for ideas.)

Conclude by discussing this quote by Mark Matlock in his book, *Raising Wise Children*: "If in my fear I refuse to allow them to participate in the technology that is now integral in daily life, I would lose the opportunity to show them how to use that technology wisely in a way that honors Christ." Pray that you would be diligent to stay on top of guiding your kids through our changing technological world.

For Additional Study

See Proverbs 4:23 for the wisdom found in "guarding our hearts."

APPLY

What I am going to do: When:

- Define some parameters for the use of social media in our home. _____

- "Friend" or "Follow my kids on their active social media sites. _____

- Establish a "family technology contract" that we all sign. _____

- Have the "digital footprint" conversation. _____

- _____ _____

- _____ _____

- _____ _____

- _____ _____

MORE

Books to Read:

From Santa to Sexting by Brenda Hunter shows how quickly our kids transition into the world of social media influence.

Emotional Purity by Heather Paulson gives an excellent overview of the reasons for "guarding your heart."

Videos to Watch:

"Being 13" is a powerful Anderson Cooper report produced by CNN about the impact of social media on our teens.

Other:

A simple Google search for *"social media monitoring for parents"* will give you some current tools to stay connected with your kids.

Search images of *"family technology contract"* for some great printable contracts your family can implement at home.

Session 4

When They're Ready to Date

"Helping your kids to date smart."

LISTEN

Start talking as early as you possibly can about what dating is going to look like in your home. You don't want to introduce guidelines for the first time when your kids are sixteen.

Some things that every parent needs to consider:

Q. What is the _____ of dating?

Q. What _____ will your kids be allowed to date?

Q. Under what _____ will you allow dating to happen?

Don't just give your kids rules without _____.

1. Help your kids understand the principle of being

_____ _____.

2. Help your kids understand the reasons for _____
boundaries.

There is a chemical compound found in all of our bodies:

_____.

   *Negative Implication #1: Sex makes you _____.

   *Negative Implication #2: Oxytocin _____ can
   take its toll.

   *The Positive Implication: Oxytocin can powerfully
              _____ a husband and wife.

3. Help your kids understand the need for

_____ involvement.

Potential _____ need to go through you first.

4. Speak openly about the sexual _____

present in any relationship.

DISCUSS

Any preparation you have done to help your kids have a healthy view of their sexuality is put to the test once they start considering their first romantic relationship. Up to this point, things have been "theoretical." Once they have some freedom (and some active hormones) they will need a great deal of coaching and leadership. That's why it is so important for parents to remain intentional during this season.

Questions to Consider

Q. What was your earliest experience with dating when you were a teenager? Was it positive or negative? Why?

Q. Discuss the three questions about your philosophy of dating found on page 27. Listen carefully to the perspective of others.

Q. Does the discussion of oxytocin give you any "aha" moments regarding any romantic relationships (both healthy and unhealthy) that you may have observed in the past?

Scripture to Examine

We should be careful not to let our kids enter romantic relationships carelessly. Christian teenagers can become easily distracted from the things of God by their boyfriends/girlfriends. It is the quickest and easiest way for our kids to develop a divided heart, something warned against time and time again in Scripture.

Take a moment to look back on the romantic relationships you had during high school. If you were a Christian during those years, reflect on the effect your boyfriends or girlfriends had on your spiritual life. If you are honest, you will probably conclude that it was a hindrance to being able to focus deeply on the things of God.

"So whether you eat or drink or whatever you do, do it all for the glory of God." –I Corinthians 10:31

Every relationship (especially romantic ones) should be entered into with a clear plan for it to enhance, not detract from, our kids' spiritual lives. Doing so requires us to equip our kids with a perspective of dating/relationships from the earliest age possible. It also requires us to share the reasons "why" for our philosophy, not just hard and fast rules that our kids are likely to reject.

Q. How might you begin to share healthy and wise perspectives of dating with your kids? (Consider the truths about oxytocin, being equally-yoked, and sexual temptation.)

Q. What are some principles you can establish for your home that will provide accountability to your kids as they begin to date?

Conclude by praying for any families who currently have kids in dating relationships. If your group is younger, talk about ways that you can begin "indoctrinating" your kids now with a healthy philosophy of dating. Be sure to remind your kids that they way your family operates may be radically different from the way other families do. And that's okay.

For Additional Study

See I Corinthians 6:18 for a clear directive on the importance of "fleeing sexual immorality."

Check out 2 Corinthians 6:14 for the principle related to being "equally yoked.

APPLY

What I am going to do: **When:**

- Try to define a philosophy of dating that help guide our decisions.   will _____

- Talk with our kids about how we will decide when they are ready to date. _____

- Do some research and have some talks about oxytocin bonding with our kids. _____

- For our teens who are currently in romantic relationships have some frank talks about guarding against sexual temptation. _____

- _____ _____

- _____ _____

MORE

Books to Read:

For Young Women Only by Shaunti Feldhahn gives teen girls a perspective on the minds of teen guys.

Hooked: New Science on How Casual Sex is Affecting our Children by McIlhaney, Jr. and Freda McKissic Bush shares about the science of oxytocin.

Interviewing Your Daughter's Date by Dennis Rainey gives parents a place to start offering accountability to their dating teens.

The New Rules for Sex, Love, and Dating by Andy Stanley should be required reading for every college age young adult.

Videos to Watch:

The music video for *Gnarls Barkley's "Who's Gonna Save My Soul"* includes a explanation of how our hearts bond with others whom we date. (Warning: it's bloody...literally.) Find it at www.youtube.com/watch?v=gUhCKFNuj3Q

Session 5

The Pornography Problem

"Equipping Your Kids to fight the new drug."

LISTEN

Pornography Defined: sexually explicit videos, photographs, writings, or the like, produced to elicit sexual arousal.

What's Wrong With Porn?

1. It devalues _____.

2. It gives an _____ picture of sex.

3. It is highly_____.

4. It trains one to be _____.

5. Frequent self-gratification can mess with one's _____.

6. It _____ the marital connection.

Parents can't afford to take this lightly.

Four Things Parents Must Do:

1. _____ your kids from an early age.

2. Give them some _____ education.

    *What the industry looks like.

    *What porn will do to you.

    *Train your kids to guard their eyes.

    *Train your kids to bounce their eyes.

3. Create appropriate _____.

4. Have frequent _____.

Most importantly, combat shame with love and acceptance.

DISCUSS

Nothing has changed the sexual landscape of our culture and negatively impacted more relationships today than pornography. While statistics show that the majority of our teenagers are consuming it at an alarming pace, we are only beginning to understand the damage it is causing. Unfortunately, we may not fully know its devastation on an entire generation until the teenagers who have consumed it through their developmental years enter into marriage.

Questions to Consider

Q. Did watching the video trouble you (more than you already were) regarding the pornography problem? Why or why not?

Q. Do you know anyone personally whose life or relationship has been negatively affected by pornography? Without giving names or specific details, be willing to share their story.

Q. On a scale of 1-10, how equipped do you feel to help your kids make wise choices regarding explicit material?

Scripture to Examine

While pornography and masturbation are not mentioned in the Bible, Jesus tells us in no uncertain terms that lust is a serious sin. We can confidently assume that His words have specific application to the prolific availability of porn in our world today.

"Anyone who looks at a woman lustfully has already committed adultery with her in his heart." –Matthew 5:28

I have yet to find anyone who can view porn without lusting. As with every other sin, Jesus is reminding us that lust has significant consequences on our relationships with others. It's about time that we started believing Him. We must take this sin seriously and take whatever steps we can to help our kids remain free from the lure of porn and sexual addiction.

Q. Why do you think parents tend to be passive about an issue that God takes so seriously?

Q. How can sexual sin in our own lives or in our past negatively impact our ability to help our kids?

We must respond to the pornography problem by being diligent to educate, train, and safeguard our kids. While parents might want a magic bullet that will make this problem go away, it simply doesn't exist. There are a number of resources mentioned in the "MORE" section below, but no tool will take the place of open and honest conversations about the dangers of porn and God's offer of a better way. We must get comfortable talking about this issue!

Conclude your small group time by praying for wisdom to know how to guard and protect your kids as well as courage to have these conversations. Pray that God would give your kids the conviction to do the right thing even when no one is looking.

For Additional Study

In Job 31:1, we find a great verse to memorize. Job essentially declares that he is making a covenant with his eyes not to lust.

Check out Romans 8:1 for a reminder that shaming another believer for sexual sin is not the way of Jesus. Parents can apply this to how they respond to their kids caught in sin.

APPLY

What I am going to do:	When:
• Use filtering software and adjust device settings to limit accessibility to porn.	_____
• Have a detailed age-appropriate conversation with your kids about how they should respond when they encounter porn.	_____
• Offer help and grace to any of our kids who we know has struggled with porn.	_____
• _____	_____
• _____	_____
• _____	_____

MORE

Books to Read:

Good Pictures/Bad Pictures is a book for younger children that equips them to respond wisely should they encounter porn.

Preparing Your son for Every Young Man's Battle by Steven Arterburn is a valuable tool for parents of tweens.

Every Young Man's Battle by Steven Arterburn is a great read for older teens.

Every Young Woman's Battle by Shannon Ethridge approaches this subject from a female perspective.

Videos To Watch:

The Conqueror's DVD Series offers a battle plan for men struggling with porn addiction.

TED Talks have a few presentations related to the negative affects of pornography. (Watch with discretion; they can be explicit.)

Two recent Hollywood movies effectively address porn addiction. *"Don John"* **and** *"Thanks for Sharing"* are (secular) movies that show the negative affects of porn. They are both rated R (for good reason) but might give helpful insights for adults.

Other:

Circle is a new device that enables you to wirelessly monitor every device connected to the WiFi of your home. It is a powerful tool that might be helpful.

BSecure Online, X3Watch, and Covenant Eyes are just a few effective computer monitoring options. Compare what is available and choose the one that is best for your family.

Most smartphone operating systems now have **password-protected filters that block adult content.** No teenager should have a phone where those are not activated.

Brain Buddy is a smartphone app designed to help re-train the brain to break free from porn addiction. (Along with God and community, brain training is the 3rd necessary component of any strategy to have victory over porn addiction.)

Session 6

Discovering A Better Way

"Preparing Our Kids to Get This Right"

LISTEN

For many people, sexuality is the source of their greatest brokenness. Given that God made sex for our good, this is one of the greatest tragedies on Earth.

Our kids don't see many examples of "a better way."

Parents must make every effort to frame the conversation, not just respond.

How do we offer a better way to our kids?

*Don't teach what's wrong with sex. Teach what is

_____ about it.

*Teach your boys how to be _____.

*Teach your girls to be _____.

*Teach your kids how to be _____ in relationships.

*Teach your kids about _____ the right person.

Conclusion - There's bad news and good news:

The Bad News:

You (and your kids) are going to _____ _____.

The Good News:

The _____ _____ _____ always offers us a fresh start and a new life.

DISCUSS

While most parents are diligent to prepare their kids to be successful in academics, sports, and character development, few take the time to prepare their kids to eventually have a healthy marriage. They forget that the developmental childhood and teen years are the best time to help them to prepare. To do this successfully, parents must stop being reactive and start being proactive in equipping their kids to navigate a hyper-sexualized culture.

Questions to Consider

Q. When your parents taught you about sexual behaviors as a teen, was the focus more on what's bad about sex or what's good about it? Why does it matter?

Q. What are some examples of the lack of chivalry and modesty in our kids' generation?

Q. Why are we so apt to believe that we are cursed forever with the consequences of our poor sexual decisions? Why do you think it is so hard to break free from their hold on our hearts and minds?

Scripture to Examine

If we are going to offer our kids a better way for their future marriages, we must believe that there is hope for restoration from some of our worst sexual failures. We must also offer this hope to them when they mess up. Paul writes about this in numerous places, but it is beautifully summed up in Colossians 1:21-22:

"Although you were formerly alienated and hostile in mind, engaged in evil deeds, yet He has now reconciled you in His fleshly body through death, in order to present you before Him holy and blameless and beyond reproach."

Because of the cross, the believer's identity is no longer as a sinner, but as one who stands holy and pure before God. So much Christian teaching on sexual sin misses this truth altogether. It's as if sexual mistakes are unforgiveable and the perpetrator is forever "damaged goods." This thinking goes against everything that the gospel of Jesus Christ teaches.

We read in 2 Corinthians 5:17 that *"If anyone is in Christ, he is a new creation; the old has passed away; behold the new has come."* If this isn't true for all of our sin, it's not true for any of it. When we feel that this doesn't apply to sexual brokenness, we're selling the gospel short. Christ-followers must choose to walk in the forgiveness and freedom that God so freely offers.

Q. If we believe that God forgives our sexual past, why do you think we continue to struggle with it so? Is it because it so powerfully impacts our relationships?

Q. How does brokenness from your own past motivate you to want to help your kids to walk in God's better way for their relationships?

Since this is the last session of the study, conclude your time by reflecting on some of your biggest takeaways. Articulate what you are going to differently as a result of processing through these truths. Be willing to share some of the "ACTION STEPS" from previous sections that have been the most significant for you.

End with prayer, asking God to lead every family in your group to look to Him for help and guidance in the coming days.

For Additional Study

Read Proverbs 5:18 to see God's enthusiastic endorsement of sex in marriage.

Matthew 19:5 is pretty good, as well!

APPLY

What I am going to do: When:

- Start training my son to be chivalrous.   _____

- Start teaching my daughter how to be
  feminine, modest, and virtuous.   _____

- Help my kids to get a vision for being the
  right kind of husband or wife one day.   _____

- Offer tons of grace to my kids for past
  mistakes in the sexual realm.   _____

- Personally bask in the tons of grace that
  God offers to you for your past mistakes.   _____

- _____   _____

- _____   _____

MORE

Books to Read:

What He Must Be to Marry My Daughter by Voddie Baucham
sets the bar pretty high for helping your kids find the right spouse.

Raising a Modern Day Knight by Robert Lewis gives an excellent
call to chivalry.

Developmental Appendix:
A General Guide for Every Age

What Every Kindergartener
Needs to Know About Sex

Don't let that title shock you. I am not advocating for traditional sex-ed for preschoolers. Far from it. What I hope to do is encourage parents to start very early to build the framework for helping their kids to have the right perspective on the sexual aspect of their lives.

In our ministry of equipping parents to help their kids make wise choices about sex and relationships, we like to use the concept of "navigating." Just as a rafting guide helps people to navigate the hazards that are always part of a whitewater adventure, a parent's job is to help their kids to successfully get through the many relational and sexual challenges that every person will encounter.

Helping parents to do that job right is the reason that we wrote The Talks and filmed this DVD series. In our hyper-sexualized culture, we're amazed at how many parents haven't given any thought whatsoever regarding how they will help their kids to have a healthy view of sex.

When it comes to these issues, parents of preschoolers should see their job as one of building the right foundation. To stay with the whitewater rafting illustration, a guide must make sure everyone on his boat can swim long before he lets them get close to the water.

If the goal is to lay a solid foundation for your preschoolers, this list should probably be titled something a little more broad, such as "What Every Kindergartner Needs to Know About Their Bodies, Their Sexuality, and the Opposite Sex."

Note that this is not an exhaustive list. And it shouldn't serve as a legalistic checklist. But by the time he or she finishes kindergarten your child should be able to have some awareness of the following:

1. The opposite sex does not have "cooties." They are different, but they are awesome.

2. Mom and dad will honestly (and simply) answer questions I have about the different parts of my body without making me feel shame about them.

3. My body belongs to me. Nobody can touch me without my permission. More specifically, I need to carefully guard the parts of my body that are covered by a bathing suit. If anyone every touches me in a way I don't like, I know I can tell my parents. They are there to protect me.

4. Kisses are special and need to be saved for the people who have spent a lifetime meriting such special affection.

5. Mom and dad love me so much that they put a filter on the internet that keeps me from stumbling into something that I don't need to see.

6. If I happen to see someone with their clothes off, I need to look away. Private parts are meant to be kept private.

7. My parents give me a good picture of what a healthy and affectionate marriage looks like. Even if they are single, they make me feel secure by their relationship choices.

8. My parents care enough about me to begin thinking now about how to create a framework for me to develop a healthy view of my sexuality.

What Every Elementary School Kid Needs to Know About Sex

Don't freak out. Your 4th grader may not need to know a bunch of explicit details about how sex works. But by the time they are 9 or 10 (every kid is different), they probably need to know some "birds and bees" basics. In addition, elementary school is the perfect season for your kids to begin to develop a healthy perspective of the way God has made them uniquely male or female. They also need loving and wise parents who will protect them from some of the pitfalls that our over-sexualized culture will begin to put in their paths.

Our kids will face these issues long before we think, so we cannot afford to put this off. All it takes is one conversation on the playground or one glimpse of something on the computer to give our kids the wrong impression of something God made to be a wonderful thing.

Parents of elementary kids should begin to give their kids a healthy impression of sex. To stay with the whitewater rafting illustration given in the previous section about kindergarteners, a guide will make sure that the tourists on his boat have a positive perspective of what they are about to encounter on the river. He wants them to know that it might be a bit scary, but it's going to be awesome.

With the goal of putting a positive spin on sex and relationships, this list should probably be titled something a little more broad, such as "What Every Elementary School Kid Needs to Know About Their Bodies, Their Sexuality, and the Opposite Sex."

This is not an exhaustive list. And it shouldn't serve as a legalistic checklist. But by the time he completes the 4th grade, your child should be able to have some awareness of the following:

1. "Everything that a Kindergartener Needs to Know," plus...

2. The basics of "where babies come from." I will develop plenty of questions over time, but I have heard about intercourse from my parents before I hear it somewhere else.

3. God invented sex to connect a husband and wife, to make babies, AND to be something that feels good to us. Though it is a bit bizarre, my parents have told me that it truly is a wonderful thing. (I'm still not convinced.)

4. I know that, while God made sex and our bodies to be private, there are some who let people take their pictures with their clothes off. I might accidentally see these on a computer or smartphone. If this happens, I need to look away and tell my parents. They will not be mad at me.

5. My parents have trained me to notice good character qualities in members of the opposite sex. After all, I will probably get married some day and I need to learn what traits are most important in others.

6. For Girls: Because I have already started comparing myself to others, my parents remind me often that I am both beautiful and of great value beyond my looks.

7. For Boys: I am being taught how to be chivalrous, seeing the importance of using my strength to protect the young and innocent and to assist anyone who might need my help.

8. Our family may not embrace dating or boyfriends/girlfriends the same way as everyone else we know.

9. I know that if anyone makes me feel uncomfortable in a way that they talk to me or touch me, I can ALWAYS tell my parents.

10. I can regularly see my parents modeling a strong, thriving, and affectionate marriage. Even if they are single, they are making relationship choices that are best for me

What Every Pre-Teen
Needs to Know About Sex

When parents ask us when they should talk to their kids about sex, our knee-jerk answer is "sooner than you think." By the time your kids hit 5th or 6th grade, they should have a basic knowledge of the birds and the bees, but the conversation doesn't stop there. There is so much more that you and your kids need to talk about.

One tip we often give is to make sure your kids hear about terms and issues related to human sexuality before they hear them from somewhere else.

When it comes to these issues, parents of preteens should make it their goal to inform their kids of what they will likely encounter as they get older. Sadly, that might mean "stealing their innocence" and telling them about some stuff before you might be fully comfortable with it. To visit our whitewater rafting illustration once again, a guide is wise to give solid and specific information about what the journey down the river will be like long before they put the boat in the water.

With that in mind, this list has to cover more than just sex. It should probably be titled something like "What Every Pre-Teen Needs to Know About Their Bodies, Their Sexuality, and the Opposite Sex."

This is not an exhaustive list. And it shouldn't serve as a legalistic checklist. But by the time he or she finishes the 6th grade, your child should be able to have some awareness of the following:

1. "Everything that an Elementary School Kid Needs to Know About Sex," plus...

2. By this time, my parents and I have had "the talk." Though it can sometimes feel weird, I feel relatively comfortable asking my

parents the variety of strange questions that pop into my head about this topic.

3. My parents have given me some resources to look at on my own that deal with human sexuality and some of the physical changes that I can expect in the coming years.

4. I am beginning to learn that the world's perspective of sex is radically different than what God designed it to be. I am learning to trust that God's ways are best.

5. I know that when I do eventually start to date, it will be with people my parents are comfortable with. My parents will want to personally know any potential boyfriends and girlfriends. Those I date will share my religious faith.

6. Girls: I may not mature at the same pace as the girls around me, but my parents have prepared me for this. I know what changes in my body I can expect, especially as it relates to having a period.

7. Boys: I am learning more and more what it means to guard and protect women. Even though many of my friends don't seem to honor the girls around them, I am trying hard to be a gentleman in both my words and actions.

8. My parents diligently monitor my technology use to make sure I am making wise choices. They know the passwords to any sites I frequent.

9. I am learning that sex should be saved for marriage because it serves as an amazing super-glue in that relationship. I may not understand this for many years, but I was introduced to this truth by my parents early on.

10. My parents are still very affectionate, even though they are getting older. That's weird and sometimes gross, but it makes me feel oddly secure.

What Every Middle Schooler
Needs to Know About Sex

Middle school kids are seeing more and learning more about human sexuality than we ever did when we were their age. Because they will be bombarded with a worldview from so many different directions, parents cannot afford to sit by and then play catch up later.

Many kids are well into their adolescent years before their parents communicate anything substantive about their sexuality and the struggles they might face. Plenty more parents avoid these talks altogether.

When it comes to these issues, parents of middle school kids should see their role as one of "trainer." You want to equip your kids with the skills they will need get through the coming years when their sexuality becomes a more pronounced part of their lives. To stay with the whitewater rafting illustration, a guide has to train his rafters on how to get down the river without getting seriously hurt. If they are going to enjoy the journey, it is up to the guide to equip them with what they will need.

With that in mind, this list should probably be titled something a little more broad, such as "What Every Middle Schooler Needs to Know About Their Bodies, Their Sexuality, and the Opposite Sex."

This is not an exhaustive list. And it shouldn't serve as a legalistic checklist. But by the time he or she finishes the 8th grade, your child should be able to have some awareness of the following:

1. "Everything that a Pre-Teen Needs to Know About Sex," plus...

2. I am learning to interact with the opposite sex in ways that are honoring to them. I can tell that I have a tendency to be selfish in my relationships, so I am striving to put others first.

3. While I may not be dating, my parents train me to look for what I like and value in members of the opposite sex. I'm learning to look for qualities that I might one day value in a spouse.

4. Marriage is a commitment for life. I am learning that our culturally accepted practice of cohabitation has the power to undermine long-term relationships.

5. Boys: My parents have briefed me on what a wet dream is and why it happens. I know that it is perfectly normal and that it happens to every single boy on the planet.

6. Girls: As my body develops physically, I am learning to dress in a way that doesn't advertise it to others. I value my beauty, but I want boys to know and appreciate me for more than just what I look like.

7. Instead of trying to find the right person to "like" me, I know it is more important for me to become the right person. As I grow in maturity, I will be better able to recognize the person that I need to be with.

8. I know that looking at pornography has significant power to mess me up. It is addictive, harms real intimacy with others, and trains me to have a selfish view of sex. My parents are diligently monitoring my technology and reminding me to make wise choices to make sure that I do not get ensnared by it.

9. If and when I start using social media, my parents will set some limits on its use, making sure that I don't give too much of my heart away emotionally with the opposite sex.

10. If someone wants to "date" me, my parents should be involved in the process. They care about me enough to know who I am interested in.

11. My parents will occasionally lock the door to their bedroom and tell me to go away. What could that mean? I don't want to think about it.

What Every High Schooler
Needs to Know About Sex

By the time our kids enter high school, they are fully aware of the sexual component of their lives. Even if they are somewhat "inexperienced," they still have plenty of thoughts and drives that God has placed within them. These things are very good, but if they are not managed with wisdom, they have the potential to be destructive. Parents have a God-given responsibility to help their kids to make wise choices.

Our older teenage kids are in desperate need of guidance and accountability. They need trusted adults to help them to process the many feelings and experiences they will have during these tumultuous years.

Parents of high school aged kids must see their role as coach and guide. We must have specific, detailed conversations about the issues and challenges that our kids are facing...while they are facing them. We must lead as we go. To stick with the whitewater illustration, the high school years are like being in the middle of the river with class 3 and 4 rapids coming around every bend. The guide is giving directions, instructing on what to expect and do, and helping his people to learn from their mistakes before they tackle the next challenge.

Note that whitewater rafting is both thrilling AND dangerous. Along the way, people will often get hurt: everything from sore muscles to various bumps and bruises. But everything is usually okay at the end of the day as long as there weren't any significant injuries.

In the same way, our kids are likely going to have a few emotional and spiritual bruises as they get through these years. Parents who think they can fully protect their kids from that are naive. It rarely happens. However, we can and should be diligent to try to help our kids to navigate this stage of life without too much lasting damage. Hopefully, they can then enter marriage free of significant baggage. And thankfully, the cross of Christ offers us the redemption of even our biggest mistakes.

There is a lot our kids will face and our simple goal should be to help them get through it. That said, this list should probably be titled something a little more broad, such as "What Every High Schooler Needs to Know About Sex, Dating, and the Opposite Sex."

This is not an exhaustive list. And it shouldn't serve as a legalistic checklist. But by the time he or she hits the middle of high school (and has the freedom of a driver's license), your child should have some awareness of the following:

1. "Everything that a Middle Schooler Needs to Know About Sex," plus...

2. My parents have been deliberate to communicate that sex is an incredibly beautiful gift from God. However, outside the security of marriage, it has the power to ruin relationships, not make them stronger.

3. I am learning about the chemical bonds that are formed when two people connect physically. My parents have told me about the effects of "oxytocin" and how it serves as a "bonding chemical" in physically intimate relationships. Thus, I am learning not to be careless in my interaction with the opposite sex.

4. My parents have coached in some "scripts" I can use to get out of potentially tempting situations.

5. I know that it is not wise for me to be alone somewhere with someone that I am in a romantic relationship with.

6. With regard to my dating relationships, my parents are periodically asking me (and the person I am dating) about physical boundaries. They love me enough to provide accountability for us.

7. Self-gratification and the use of porn has the power to make one selfish. I know that if I get into the habit of doing that, I run the real risk of bringing a self-centered expectation of sex to my eventual marriage. This has the potential to undermine the power that sex should have to strengthen my relationship.

8. Instead of asking "how far is too far" sexually, I am asking God to show me what is the most wise thing for me to do to guard my heart, mind, and body.

9. I know that using drugs and alcohol can make me vulnerable to sexual abuse by someone who can easily take advantage of me. I am therefore very careful. I know to NEVER accept a drink that someone gives me at a party.

10. My sex drive can tempt me to think only of my needs. I am learning that God desires for me to give it generously to one person who I commit myself to for life.

11. My sexuality is more than just a physical drive. It offers a transcendent emotional and spiritual connection with another person that should not be taken lightly.

12. I will likely make some mistakes along the way as I discover God's gift of my sexuality. I will have some regrets. I will likely have emotional wounds. But I am learning that God's grace and love are sufficient to restore me and make me whole.

BARRETT AND JENIFER JOHNSON

Barrett and Jenifer founded INFO for Families in 2013 to "help regular families stay informed, equipped and on task." Popular speakers on issues related to marriage and family life, they are frequently characterized as authentic, practical, and wise. Their popular blog at *INFOforFamilies.com* averages 30,000 hits a month. Barrett has spent the past 25 years ministering to students and families through the local church, most recently serving as the Minister to Families at Johnson Ferry Baptist Church outside Atlanta, GA. They have five kids (including 3 adolescents at home) and are the youngest and coolest grandparents you know.

54906583R00038

Made in the USA
Charleston, SC
14 April 2016